Adventures With
Charlie

CHARLIE GOES TO SCHOOL

by Charles Schoen

Illustrated by Doreyl Ammons Cain

A CHILDREN'S BOOK SERIES DEDICATED TO BUILDING COMMUNITIES
THROUGH THE INCLUSION OF CHILDREN WITH SPECIAL NEEDS AND THEIR FAMILIES
THE ADAPTIVE LEARNING CENTER, MARIETTA, GEORGIA

Catch the Spirit of Appalachia, Inc.
WESTERN NORTH CAROLINA

First Edition 2014

Layout /editing by Amy Ammons Garza
Illustrated by Doreyl Ammons Cain

Publisher:

Catch the Spirit of Appalachia, Inc.—Imprint of:
Ammons Communications — SAN NO. 8 5 1 – 0 8 8 1
29 Regal Avenue • Sylva, North Carolina 28779
Phone/fax: (828) 631-4587

For additional copies of these books please go to CSAbooks.com

Library of Congress Control Number: 2014956125

ISBN No. 978-0-9908766-1-8

Dedication

This book is dedicated to
Sarah Kate and Will—
two of the best siblings
a brother could have!

Introduction

The Adventures with Charlie book series is about an inspirational boy who is not like everyone else. He is special. He magically makes friends everywhere he goes. Children need to have a story that illustrates the idea that "being different from typical peers" can have some special rewards. Parents can read a book to see the joy and special opportunities out there for families and children with special needs. In the midst of difficult challenges with raising all types of children, there are always opportunities to approach life from a different perspective which can provide joy and delight for many. It gives me great pleasure to introduce readers to "Charlie, the Prince."

Charlie, the Prince

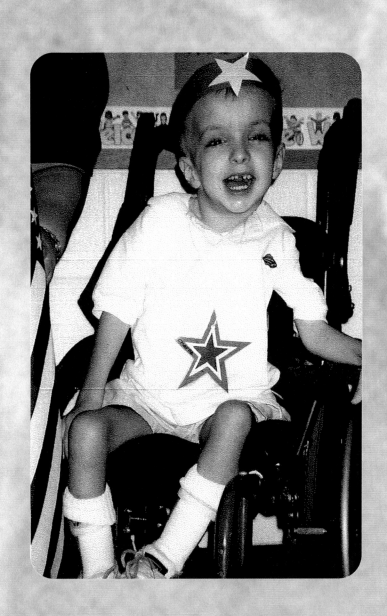

Charlie is the Prince,
who rides in a chair.

6

He has a big smile,
and bright golden hair.

Charlie has friends,
at school
and in town.

Charlie is magic,
he can fly
off the ground.

Another morning for fun, he is ready to go
to school on the bus, the fun place to grow.

He floats in the air and up he goes . . .

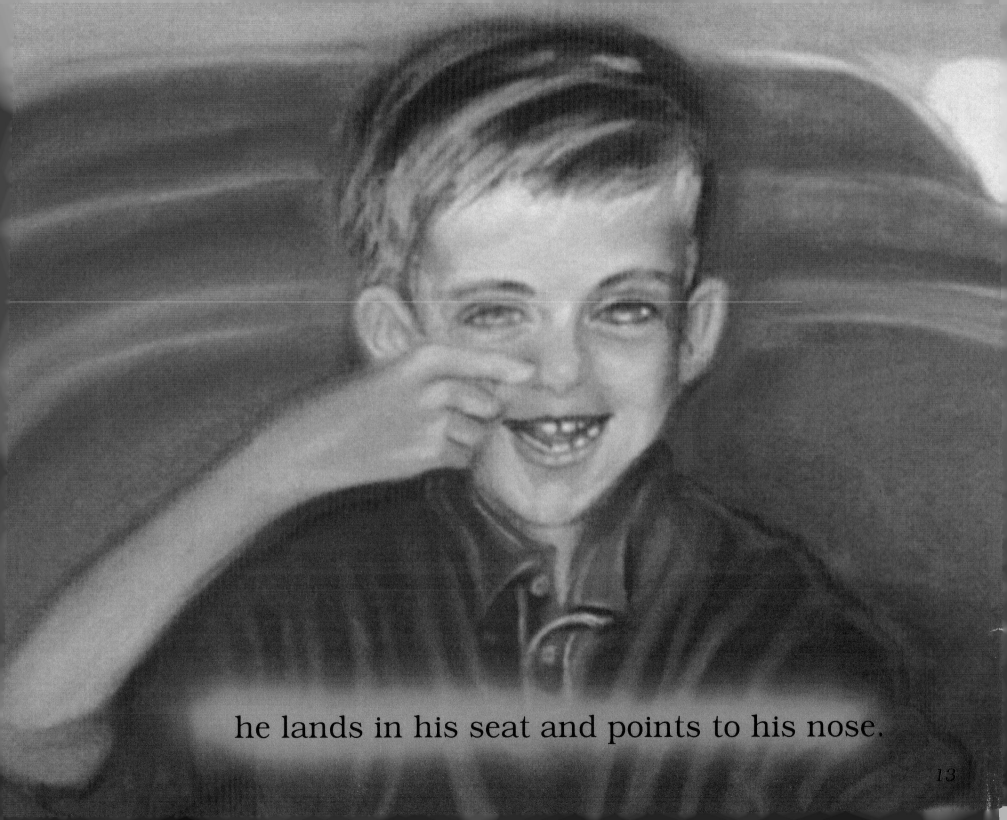

he lands in his seat and points to his nose.

Officer Combs is
waiting for him . . .

14

his favorite strong man
who escorts
him in.

First he has breakfast
all warm and yummy.

Then it is circle time and everyone's so funny!

17

The school bell rings
and Charlie changes classes.

He works on his art,
he wears his sun glasses.

18

His pictures have colors
all red, white and blue . . .
he makes them to say:
"You know I love you"

21

Lunch is his favorite—he sits with his friends
Then off to recess to play in the gyms.

22

He glides down the floor
and under the slide.

He rolls to a stop like riding the tide.

Music is next—he loves the director.

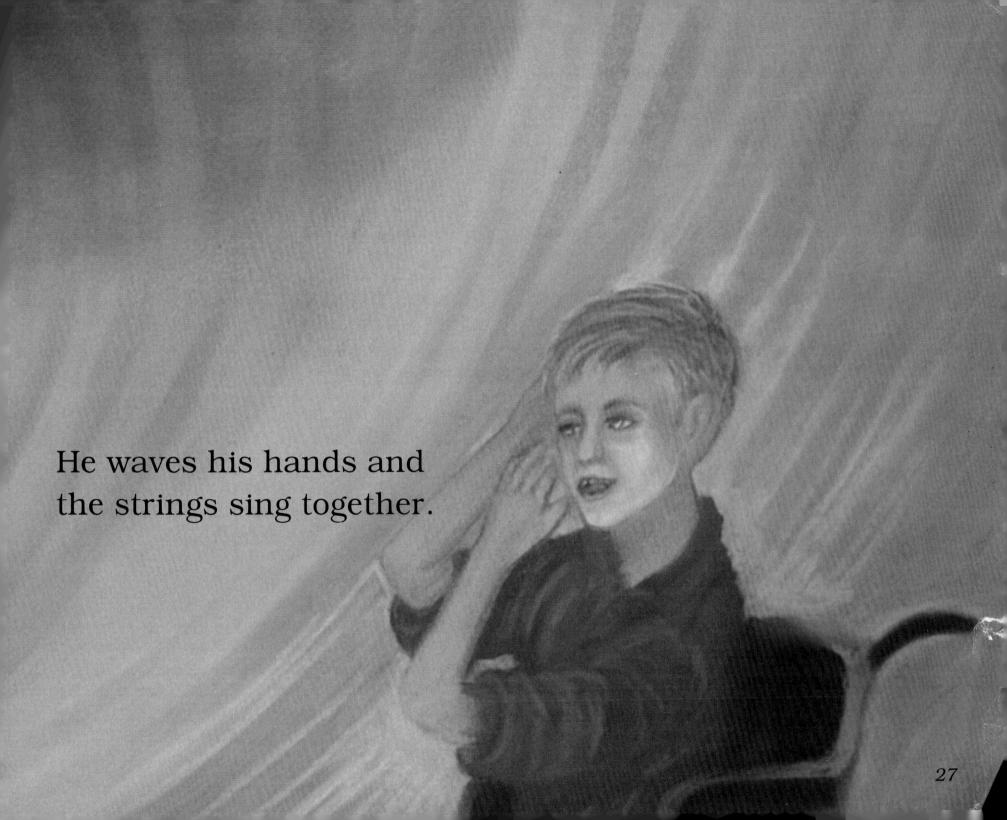

He waves his hands and
the strings sing together.

It's the end of the day and the bus comes again.

It's time to go home and *fly like the wind.*

He arrives at his house
and floats to the ground.
He says bye to Pam and
hugs her around.

Another great day Charlie has had.
He goes on inside and starts to get sad.

33

He misses his friends, he wonders where they are?

He will see them
tomorrow,
each one is a Star!

The Adaptive Learning Center

What is ALC?

We are the only organization in Georgia that fully integrates children with special needs into typical preschools – with individualized support from special education support teachers. Our partnerships with some of Atlanta's finest preschools enable children to learn and play alongside their peers in a warm and caring environment. In classes with 90 percent or more typical children, children with disabilities learn not just basic academic skills; they discover important life lessons through interactions with other children and adults.

What's the program like?

Following a thorough interview process, our staff develops customized therapy education plans that outline specific and attainable goals for each child. Using the latest strategies and intervention standards, our support teachers take a holistic approach to meeting each child's individual needs. The ALC support teacher tracks the children's progress daily and also keeps the parents informed via daily email notes. In addition, parents receive valuable guidance and documentation that helps them plan for elementary school and beyond.

What is the success rate?

With its individualized care and high education standards, ALC has been a tremendous value to families and communities for 33 years. Here proof:

- 97% of ALC children last year met 80% or more of their individualized objectives and educational goals.
- 84% of ALC children went on to typical classrooms outside of special education
- 500+ typical families served annually in more than 38 classrooms
- 80+ childhood education teachers trained in facilitation, inclusion and identification per year

For more information on ALC or having Charles and Charlie visit your school, please call 770-509-3909 or email alckids@alckids.org

www.adaptivelearningcenter.org

LOOK FOR THE NEXT BOOK IN THE SERIES "CHARLIE GOES TO TOMMY'S"